# I KNOW ABCs

ges 3+

Brighter Child®
Carson-Dellosa Publishing LLC
Greensboro, North Carolina

Brighter Child®
Carson-Dellosa Publishing LLC
PO Box 35665
Greensboro, NC 27425 USA

© 2018 Carson-Dellosa Publishing LLC. Except as permitted under the United States Copyright Act, no part of this publication may be reproduced, stored, or distributed in any form or by any means (mechanically, electronically, recording, etc.) without the prior written consent of Carson-Dellosa Publishing LLC. Brighter Child® is an imprint of Carson-Dellosa Publishing LLC.

Printed in the USA • All rights reserved.
01-162187784

ISBN 978-1-4838-4477-0

# Contents

# Uppercase A

Trace and write.

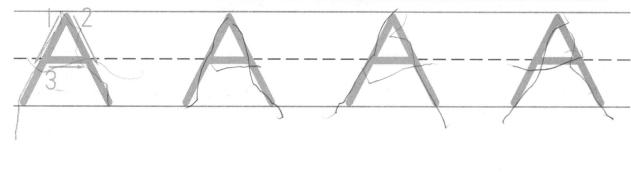

Color the apples with **A** or **a**.

# Lowercase a

Trace and write.

apples

ant

 a a a

Say each word, listening for the short **a** sound.
Circle **a** in each word.

can

map

pan

# Uppercase B

Trace and write.

Color the pictures whose names begin with the sound you hear at the beginning of **bear**.

# Lowercase b

Trace and write.

bear

bed

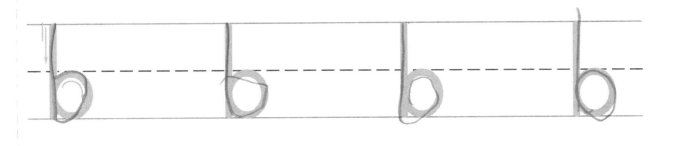

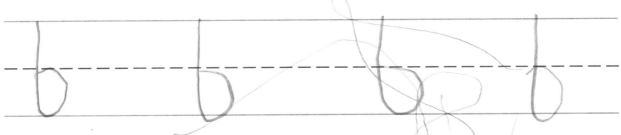

Color the **B** balloons red.
Color the **b** balloons blue.

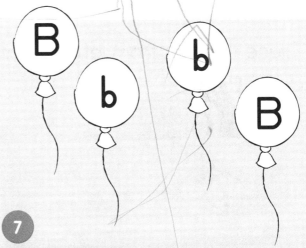

# Uppercase C

Trace and write.

C C C C C C

Trace the lines from left to right.

# Lowercase c

Trace and write.

c

cookie

cat

C   C   C   C   C

Circle the things that are cold.

# Uppercase D

Trace and write.

D D D D

Circle the objects whose names rhyme with **dog**.

# Lowercase d

Trace and write.

dog

dolphin

d     d     d     d

Follow **D** and **d** to get the dolphin to the treasure!

# Uppercase E

Trace and write.

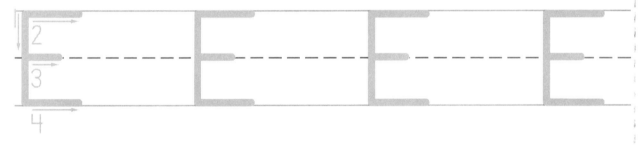

Circle the eggs with **E**.

# Lowercase e

Trace and write.

egg

elbow

e          e          e          e

Say each word, listening for the short **e** sound.
Circle **e** in each word.

tent          net          vest

# Uppercase F

Trace and write.

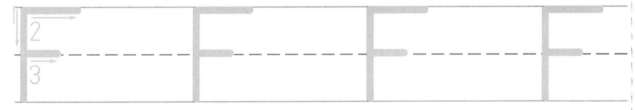

Where is the hat? Circle a word for each picture.

on
off

on

# Lowercase f

Trace and write.

fish

fork

f ——— f ——— f ——— f

- - - - - - - - - - - - - - - - - - - - -

Find and circle each **F** and **f**.

# Uppercase G

Trace and write.

G G G G

Circle the gift that
is different.

# Lowercase g

Trace and write.

g

gift

guitar

g　　　g　　　g　　　g

Color the pictures whose names begin with the sound you hear at the beginning of **gift**.

# Uppercase H

Trace and write.

Color the hearts with **H**.

# Lowercase h

Trace and write.

horse

hen

h h h h

Follow **H** and **h** to get the horse to the carrots.

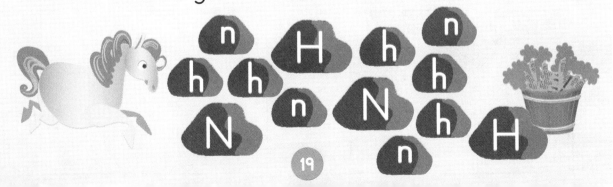

19

# Uppercase I

Trace and write.

What is the opposite of winter? Draw a picture.

# Lowercase i

Trace and write.

ice cream

igloo

Say each word, listening for the short **i** sound.
Circle **i** in each word.

bib

six

pig

# Uppercase J

Trace and write.

J J J J

Circle the word that rhymes with **jam**.

clam

drum

brush

# Lowercase j

Trace and write.

jellyfish

jam

Circle the jewels with **J** or **j**.

# Uppercase K

Trace and write.

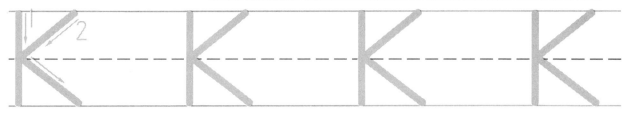

Color the picture whose name rhymes with **king**.

# Lowercase k

Trace and write.

kite

king

k ⎯ k ⎯ k ⎯ k

Color the pictures with matching letter pairs

Cc

Ak

Bb

Jg

25

# Uppercase L

Trace and write.

Color the picture whose name begins with the sound you hear at the beginning of **lion**.

# Lowercase l

Trace and write.

lemon

lion

Trace the sign.
Draw lemonade
in the glasses.

LEMONADE
25¢

# Uppercase M

Trace and write.

Circle the pictures whose names begin with the sound you hear at the beginning of **moon**.

# Lowercase m

Trace and write.

moon

monster

m    m    m    m

Find and circle each **M** and **m**.

# Uppercase N

Trace and write.

Trace the lines from left to right.

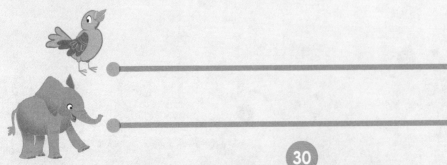

# Lowercase n

Trace and write.

nut

nest

n    n    n    n

Circle each **n**.

# Uppercase O

Trace and write.

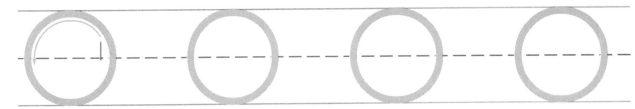

Say each word, listening for the short **o** sound.
Circle **o** in each word.

lock                box                frog

© Carson-Dellosa

Look What I Learned

I Can Do It!

Smart Cookie

Bear-y Good!

Bold & Bright

♥ It!

Turtle-ly Awesome!

Thumbs Up!

Bee-utiful

Shine On

G-r-reat

Sweet!

Paw-some!

Learning Is Fun

Toadally Cool!

High Five!

WOW!

Way to Shine!

S-S-Super

Good Job

Fantastic

Purr-fect!

© Carson-Dellosa

# Lowercase o

Trace and write.

ocean

octopus

Color the picture with a matching letter above.

c
o

o
q

o
o

# Uppercase P

Trace and write.

P P P P P

Write **P** for each penguin. Draw one more penguin in the pool.

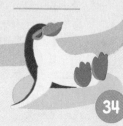

# Lowercase p

Trace and write.

penguin

popcorn

p p p p p

Circle pictures whose names begin with the sound you hear at the beginning of **penguin.**

# Uppercase Q

Trace and write.

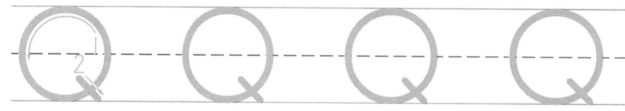

Circle the animal that **quacks**.

# Lowercase q

Trace and write.

queen

quilt

q  q  q  q

Circle the crowns with matching letter pairs.

# Uppercase R

Trace and write.

R R R R R

In each frame, draw something whose name begins with the sound you hear at the beginning of **rabbit**.

# Lowercase r

Trace and write.

rainbow

rabbit

r r r r r

Find and circle each **R** and **r**.

# Uppercase S

Trace and write.

S    S    S    S

Circle the words that rhyme with **snake**.

cake    box    hose    rake

# Lowercase s

Trace and write.

sun

sailboat

s    s    s    s

Color the suns with **S** and **s**.

# Uppercase T

Trace and write.

Trace the lines from left to right.

# Lowercase t

Trace and write.

tent

turtle

Circle the animals that can fly.

# Uppercase U

Trace and write.

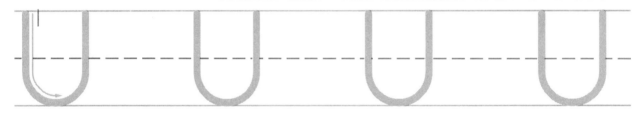

Say each word, listening for the short **u** sound. Circle **u** in each word.

tub          bus          sun

# Lowercase u

Trace and write.

umbrella

unicorn

u u u u u

Circle the word that tells where the arrow is pointing.
Find **u** in each circled word.

up

down

over

under

# Uppercase V

Trace and write.

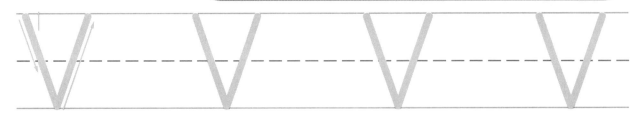

Circle pictures whose names begin with the sound you hear at the beginning of **vase**.

# Lowercase v

Trace and write.

vase

volcano

V V V V

Follow **V** and **v** to put the flowers back in the vase!

V w V x v w n v v
W v w V x v

# Uppercase W

Trace and write.

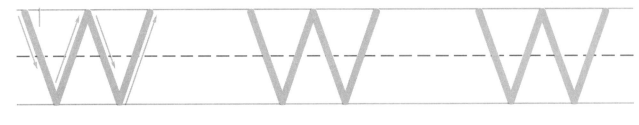

Circle the pictures with **Ww**.

# Lowercase w

Trace and write.

walrus

water

W W W W

Circle **w** in each word. Act out each word. Can a partner guess it?

wink   wave   waddle   wash

# Uppercase X

Trace and write.

X    X    X    X

**X** marks the spot! Write **X** to show where you would bury a treasure.

# Lowercase x

Trace and write.

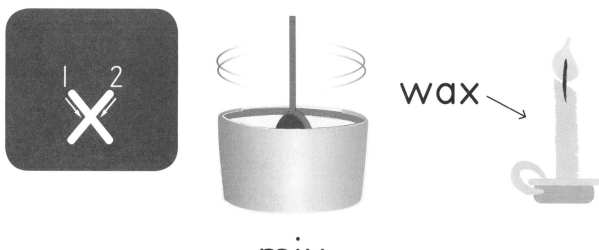

wax

mix

X X X X

Circle pictures whose names end with the sound you hear at the end of **six**.

# Uppercase Y

Trace and write.

Find two pairs of opposites.

day          wet          night          dry

# Lowercase y

Trace and write.

 yarn

yo-yo

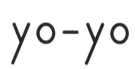

Color the picture with a matching letter pair.

Y
v

X
y

Y
Y

# Uppercase Z

Trace and write.

Circle the zoo animals. Draw a box around the farm animals.

# Lowercase z

Trace and write.

z

zebra

zigzag

z    z    z    z

Circle each **Z** and **z**.

t z Z Y k z Z z Z x

# ABC Order

Connect the dots from **A** to **Z**. Color the picture.

# ABC Order

Follow the path from **A** to **Z** to score a goal.

# ABC Order

Connect the dots from **a** to **z**. Color the picture.

# ABC Order

Follow the path from **a** to **z** to get the frog to the pond.

# Uppercase & Lowercase Letter Pairs

Match the uppercase and lowercase letters.

# Uppercase & Lowercase Letter Pairs

Match the uppercase and lowercase letters.

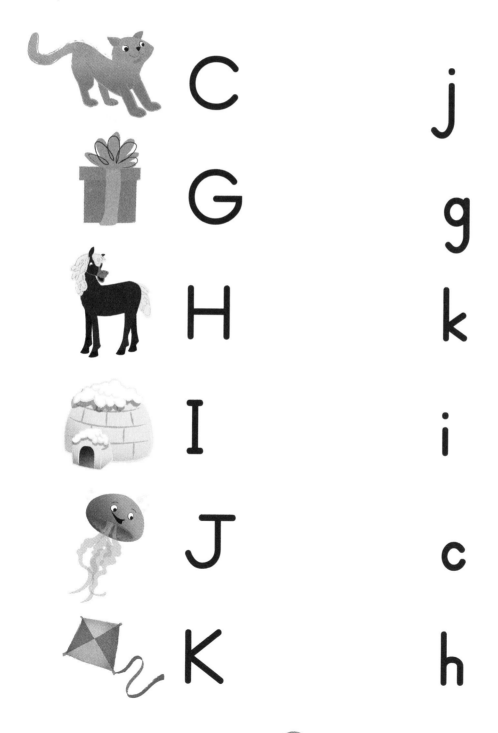

C      j

G      g

H      k

I      i

J      c

K      h

# Uppercase & Lowercase Letter Pairs

Write the missing letter in each pair.

A B

c d E

f G h

I J k

l M

# Uppercase & Lowercase Letter Pairs

Write the missing letter in each pair.

n   O   P

q   r   S

T   U   v

w   X   Y

z

# I Know the Alphabet

Find and circle the letters from **A** to **Z**.